Managing Editor
Karen Goldfluss, M.S. Ed.

Editor-in-Chief
Sharon Coan, M.S. Ed.

Cover Artist
Barb Lorseyedi

Art Coordinator
Kevin Barnes

Art Director
CJae Froshay

Imaging
James Edward Grace
Rosa C. See

Product Manager
Phil Garcia

Publishers
Rachelle Cracchiolo, M.S. Ed.
Mary Dupuy Smith, M.S. Ed.

Numbers

GRADES 3 & 4

Authors

Teacher Created Materials Staff

Teacher Created Materials, Inc.
6421 Industry Way
Westminster, CA 92683
www.teachercreated.com

ISBN-0-7439-3310-9

©*2002 Teacher Created Materials, Inc.*
Made in U.S.A.

Table of Contents

The old adage "practice makes perfect" can really hold true for your child and his or her education. The more practice and exposure your child has with concepts being taught in school, the more success he or she is likely to find. For many parents, knowing how to help their children can be frustrating because the resources may not be readily available. As a parent it is also difficult to know where to focus your efforts so that the extra practice your child receives at home supports what he or she is learning in school.

This book has been designed to help parents and teachers reinforce basic skills with their children. *Practice Makes Perfect* reviews basic math skills for children in grades 3 and 4. The math focus is on understanding numbers, the building blocks of math. While it would be impossible to include all concepts taught in grades 3 and 4 in this book, the following basic objectives are reinforced through practice exercises. These objectives support math standards established on a district, state, or national level. (Refer to the Table of Contents for the specific objectives of each practice page.)

- counting with numbers
- understanding place value
- changing expanded to standard number form
- changing standard to expanded number form
- using written, standard, and expanded forms of numbers

- reading and writing whole numbers
- comparing and ordering numbers
- identifying ordinal numbers
- rounding numbers
- identifying odd and even numbers
- writing Arabic and Roman numbers

There are 36 practice pages organized sequentially, so children can build their knowledge from more basic skills to higher-level math skills. (**Note:** Have children show all work where computation is necessary to solve a problem. For multiple-choice responses on practice pages, children can fill in the letter choice or circle the answer.) Following the practice pages are six practice tests. These provide children with multiple-choice test items to help prepare them for standardized tests administered in schools. As your child completes each test, he or she should fill in the correct bubbles on the Answer Sheet (page 46). To correct the test pages and the practice pages in this book, use the Answer Key provided on pages 47 and 48.

How to Make the Most of This Book

Here are some useful ideas for optimizing the practice pages in this book:

- Set aside a specific place in your home to work on the practice pages. Keep it neat and tidy with materials on hand.
- Set up a certain time of day to work on the practice pages. This will establish consistency. An alternative is to look for times in your day or week that are less hectic and conducive to practicing skills.
- Keep all practice sessions with your child positive and constructive. If the mood becomes tense, or you and your child are frustrated, set the book aside and look for another time to practice with your child.
- Help with instructions if necessary. If your child is having difficulty understanding what to do or how to get started, work the first problem through with him or her.
- Review the work your child has done. This serves as reinforcement and provides further practice.
- Allow your child to use whatever writing instruments he or she prefers. For example, colored pencils can add variety and pleasure to drill work.
- Pay attention to the areas in which your child has the most difficulty. Provide extra guidance and exercises in those areas. Allowing children to use drawings and manipulatives, such as coins, tiles, game markers, or flash cards, can help them grasp difficult concepts more easily.
- Look for ways to make real-life application to the skills being reinforced.

Practice 1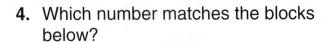

1. Which number matches the blocks below?

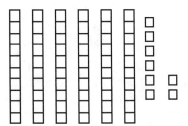

(A) 68   (B) 86   (C) 85   (D) 69

2. Which number matches the blocks below?

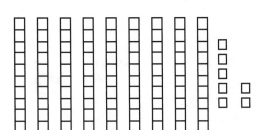

(A) 97   (B) 80   (C) 79   (D) 98

3. Which number matches the blocks below?

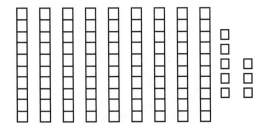

(A) 90   (B) 99   (C) 98   (D) 89

4. Which number matches the blocks below?

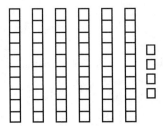

(A) 64   (B) 46   (C) 63   (D) 45

5. Which number matches the blocks below?

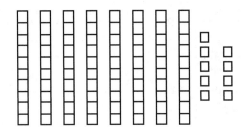

(A) 97   (B) 98   (C) 89   (D) 88

6. Which number matches the blocks below?

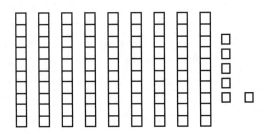

(A) 69   (B) 96   (C) 95   (D) 70

Practice 2

1. Which number matches the blocks below?

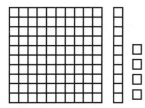

(A) 114   (B) 115   (C) 141   (D) 140

2. Which number matches the blocks below?

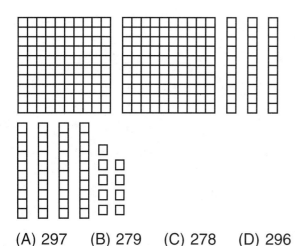

(A) 297   (B) 279   (C) 278   (D) 296

3. Which number matches the blocks below?

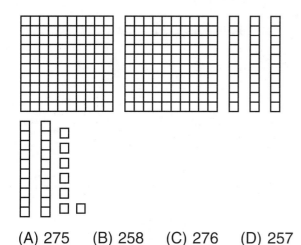

(A) 275   (B) 258   (C) 276   (D) 257

4. Which number matches the blocks below?

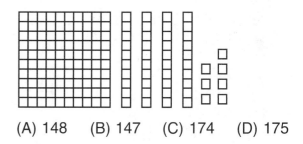

(A) 148   (B) 147   (C) 174   (D) 175

5. Which number matches the blocks below?

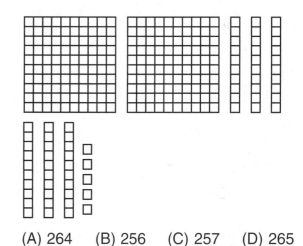

(A) 264   (B) 256   (C) 257   (D) 265

6. Which number matches the blocks below?

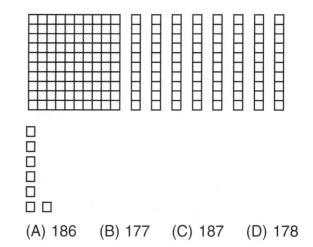

(A) 186   (B) 177   (C) 187   (D) 178

Practice 3

Write the number that each set of blocks represents.

1. _____

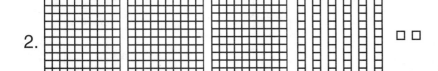

2. _____

3. _____

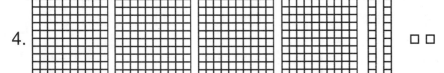

4. _____

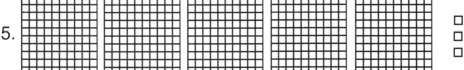

5. _____

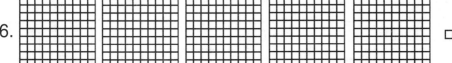

6. _____

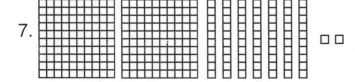

7. _____

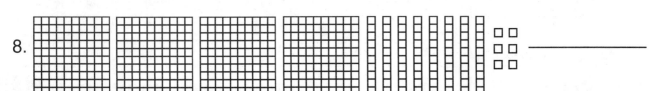

8. _____

Practice 4

Look at the number blocks. Complete the place value charts.

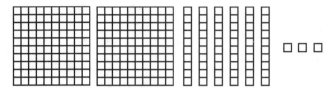

1.

hundreds	tens	ones

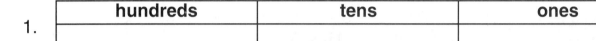

2.

hundreds	tens	ones

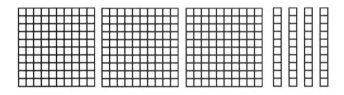

3.

hundreds	tens	ones

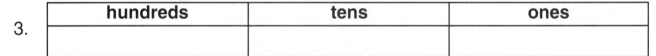

4.

hundreds	tens	ones

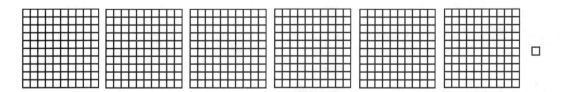

5.

hundreds	tens	ones

Practice 5

1. What place value does the digit 9 have in 9,856?

   (A) nine hundreds   (B) thousands   (C) ones   (D) tens

---

2. What place value does the digit 8 have in 2,598?

   (A) ones   (B) hundreds   (C) zeros   (D) thousands

---

3. What place value does the digit 8 have in 7,689?

   (A) eights   (B) hundreds   (C) thousands   (D) tens

---

4. What place value does the digit 4 have in 6,472?

   (A) ones   (B) twenties   (C) hundreds   (D) tens

---

5. What place value does the digit 3 have in 4,037?

   (A) thousands   (B) threes   (C) hundreds   (D) tens

---

6. What place value does the digit 5 have in 3,725?

   (A) thousands   (B) ones   (C) hundreds   (D) zeros

---

7. What place value does the digit 2 have in 5,264?

   (A) zeros   (B) ones   (C) hundreds   (D) tens

---

8. What place value does the digit 8 have in 2,083?

   (A) tens   (B) thousands   (C) hundreds   (D) eights

---

9. What place value does the digit 2 have in 6,342?

   (A) hundreds   (B) ones   (C) thousands   (D) zeros

---

10. What place value does the digit 9 have in 8,539?

    (A) ones   (B) thousands   (C) hundreds   (D) zeros

Practice 6

1. What is the value of the digit 7 in the number 2,457?

   (A) 7   (B) 1   (C) 70   (D) 700

2. What is the value of the digit 9 in the number 6,983?

   (A) 900   (B) 9,000   (C) 9   (D) 100

3. What is the value of the digit 7 in the number 2,579?

   (A) 700   (B) 70   (C) 10   (D) 7,000

4. What is the value of the digit 6 in the number 6,384?

   (A) 6   (B) 60   (C) 6,000   (D) 1,000

5. What is the value of the digit 3 in the number 2,793?

   (A) 30   (B) 300   (C) 1   (D) 3

6. What is the value of the digit 4 in the number 6,485?

   (A) 4   (B) 100   (C) 400   (D) 4,000

7. What is the value of the digit 3 in the number 2,934?

   (A) 3,000   (B) 10   (C) 300   (D) 30

8. What is the value of the digit 6 in the number 6,587?

   (A) 60   (B) 6,000   (C) 1,000   (D) 6

9. What is the value of the digit 5 in the number 2,345?

   (A) 500   (B) 5   (C) 50   (D) 1

10. What is the value of the digit 7 in the number 6,789?

    (A) 100   (B) 7,000   (C) 7   (D) 700

Practice 7

1. In 329,786, what digit tells the number of ones?

2. In 786,925, what digit tells the number of thousands?

3. In 642,379, what digit tells the number of tens?

4. In 546,379, what digit tells the number of ten thousands?

5. In 738,256, what digit tells the number of hundreds?

6. In 527,349, what digit tells the number of hundred thousands?

7. In 835,492, what digit tells the number of hundreds?

8. In 265,379, what digit tells the number of thousands?

9. In 348,276, what digit tells the number of ten thousands?

10. In 687,259, what digit tells the number of hundred thousands?

11. In 837,462 the digit 4 is in what place?

12. In 562,479 the digit 9 is in what place?

13. In 245,967 the digit 6 is in what place?

14. In 673,854 the digit 7 is in what place?

15. In 623,758 the digit 3 is in what place?

16. In 785,629 the digit 7 is in what place?

17. In 587,329 the digit 8 is in what place?

18. In 675,492 the digit 2 is in what place?

19. In 796,358 the digit 5 is in what place?

20. In 246,973 the digit 2 is in what place?

Practice 8

1. Write 300 + 40 + 9 in standard form.
   - (A) 394
   - (B) 430
   - (C) 349
   - (D) 943

2. Write 100 + 20 + 3 in standard form.
   - (A) 321
   - (B) 132
   - (C) 150
   - (D) 123

3. Write 400 + 70 + 8 in standard form.
   - (A) 874
   - (B) 478
   - (C) 550
   - (D) 487

4. Write 600 + 80 + 2 in standard form.
   - (A) 682
   - (B) 628
   - (C) 286
   - (D) 700

5. Write 500 + 90 + 4 in standard form.
   - (A) 630
   - (B) 594
   - (C) 549
   - (D) 495

6. Write 800 + 20 + 5 in standard form.
   - (A) 870
   - (B) 852
   - (C) 825
   - (D) 528

7. Write 200 + 30 + 6 in standard form.
   - (A) 263
   - (B) 632
   - (C) 290
   - (D) 236

8. Write 400 + 50 + 2 in standard form.
   - (A) 254
   - (B) 470
   - (C) 452
   - (D) 425

9. Write 800 + 70 + 6 in standard form.
   - (A) 678
   - (B) 867
   - (C) 876
   - (D) 930

10. Write 200 + 40 + 9 in standard form.
    - (A) 249
    - (B) 942
    - (C) 330
    - (D) 294

11. Write 300 + 80 + 7 in standard form.
    - (A) 450
    - (B) 378
    - (C) 387
    - (D) 783

12. Write 100 + 20 + 8 in standard form.
    - (A) 200
    - (B) 821
    - (C) 182
    - (D) 128

13. Write 700 + 40 + 2 in standard form.
    - (A) 724
    - (B) 760
    - (C) 742
    - (D) 247

14. Write 600 + 30 + 5 in standard form.
    - (A) 536
    - (B) 653
    - (C) 680
    - (D) 635

15. Write 800 + 50 + 9 in standard form.
    - (A) 958
    - (B) 859
    - (C) 940
    - (D) 895

16. Write 200 + 70 + 3 in standard form.
    - (A) 273
    - (B) 300
    - (C) 372
    - (D) 237

17. Write 900 + 20 + 7 in standard form.
    - (A) 990
    - (B) 927
    - (C) 972
    - (D) 729

18. Write 300 + 40 + 8 in standard form.
    - (A) 420
    - (B) 384
    - (C) 348
    - (D) 843

Practice 9

1. Write $500,000 + 20,000 + 7,000 + 600 + 20 + 9$ in standard form.
   (A) 5,027,629   (B) 527,692   (C) 527,629   (D) 5,276,029

2. Write $900,000 + 40,000 + 3,000 + 500 + 80 + 6$ in standard form.
   (A) 9,043,586   (B) 9,435,086   (C) 943,568   (D) 943,586

3. Write $400,000 + 4,000 + 100 + 10 + 5$ in standard form.
   (A) 4,041,015   (B) 44,115   (C) 404,151   (D) 404,115

4. Write $100,000 + 70,000 + 7,000 + 800 + 40 + 8$ in standard form.
   (A) 177,848   (B) 1,778,048   (C) 1,077,848   (D) 177,884

5. Write $300,000 + 90,000 + 6,000 + 300 + 30 + 2$ in standard form.
   (A) 396,323   (B) 3,096,332   (C) 396,332   (D) 3,963,032

6. Write $700,000 + 20,000 + 1,000 + 600 + 50 + 9$ in standard form.
   (A) 7,216,059   (B) 721,659   (C) 721,695   (D) 7,021,659

7. Write $200,000 + 40,000 + 2,000 + 500 + 30 + 8$ in standard form.
   (A) 242,583   (B) 242,538   (C) 2,425,038   (D) 2,042,538

8. Write $600,000 + 1,000 + 100 + 70 + 4$ in standard form.
   (A) 601,147   (B) 601,174   (C) 6,011,074   (D) 61,174

9. Write $800,000 + 70,000 + 6,000 + 800 + 50 + 9$ in standard form.
   (A) 876,859   (B) 8,076,859   (C) 8,768,059   (D) 876,895

10. Write $500,000 + 90,000 + 1,000 + 300 + 50 + 2$ in standard form.
    (A) 5,091,352   (B) 5,913,052   (C) 591,352   (D) 591,325

Practice 10

1. Write 40,000 + 5,000 + 300 + 50 + 8 in standard form.

_____

2. Write 20,000 + 8,000 + 900 + 60 + 5 in standard form.

_____

3. Write 60,000 + 4,000 + 700 + 40 + 7 in standard form.

_____

4. Write 90,000 + 6,000 + 500 + 70 + 6 in standard form.

_____

5. Write 70,000 + 8,000 + 300 + 90 + 9 in standard form.

_____

6. Write 50,000 + 9,000 + 200 + 30 + 2 in standard form.

_____

7. Write 20,000 + 4,000 + 600 + 20 + 3 in standard form.

_____

8. Write 70,000 + 3,000 + 800 + 80 + 4 in standard form.

_____

9. Write 60,000 + 2,000 + 900 + 70 + 3 in standard form.

_____

10. Write 50,000 + 7,000 + 300 + 90 + 6 in standard form.

Practice 11

1. Write 432 in expanded form.
    (A) 400 + 30 + 20
    (B) 400 + 30 + 2
    (C) 200 + 30 + 4
    (D) 400 + 20 + 3

6. Write 679 in expanded form.
    (A) 900 + 70 + 6
    (B) 600 + 70 + 90
    (C) 600 + 70 + 9
    (D) 600 + 90 + 7

2. Write 975 in expanded form.
    (A) 900 + 70 + 50
    (B) 900 + 70 + 5
    (C) 500 + 70 + 9
    (D) 900 + 50 + 7

7. Write 956 in expanded form.
    (A) 900 + 60 + 5
    (B) 900 + 50 + 6
    (C) 600 + 50 + 9
    (D) 900 + 50 + 60

3. Write 289 in expanded form.
    (A) 900 + 80 + 2
    (B) 200 + 90 + 8
    (C) 200 + 80 + 90
    (D) 200 + 80 + 9

8. Write 548 in expanded form.
    (A) 500 + 80 + 4
    (B) 500 + 40 + 8
    (C) 800 + 40 + 5
    (D) 500 + 40 + 80

4. Write 593 in expanded form.
    (A) 300 + 90 + 5
    (B) 500 + 30 + 9
    (C) 500 + 90 + 30
    (D) 500 + 90 + 3

9. Write 364 in expanded form.
    (A) 300 + 40 + 6
    (B) 400 + 60 + 3
    (C) 300 + 60 + 40
    (D) 300 + 60 + 4

5. Write 465 in expanded form.
    (A) 500 + 60 + 4
    (B) 400 + 60 + 50
    (C) 400 + 60 + 5
    (D) 400 + 50 + 6

10. Write 476 in expanded form.
    (A) 400 + 60 + 7
    (B) 600 + 70 + 4
    (C) 400 + 70 + 60
    (D) 400 + 70 + 6

Practice 12

1. Write 1,524 in expanded form.
    (A) 15,000 + 200 + 40
    (B) 10,000 + 5,000 + 20 + 4
    (C) 1,000 + 50 + 5
    (D) 1,000 + 500 + 20 + 4

2. Write 6,769 in expanded form.
    (A) 67,000 + 600 + 90
    (B) 6,000 + 700 + 60 + 9
    (C) 60,000 + 7,000 + 60 + 9
    (D) 6,000 + 70 + 7

3. Write 2,887 in expanded form.
    (A) 2,000 + 80 + 8
    (B) 28,000 + 800 + 70
    (C) 20,000 + 8,000 + 80 + 7
    (D) 2,000 + 800 + 80 + 7

4. Write 4,935 in expanded form.
    (A) 4,000 + 90 + 9
    (B) 49,000 + 300 + 50
    (C) 40,000 + 9,000 + 30 + 5
    (D) 4,000 + 900 + 30 + 5

5. Write 3,316 in expanded form.
    (A) 3,000 + 30 + 3
    (B) 30,000 + 3,000 + 10 + 6
    (C) 33,000 + 100 + 60
    (D) 3,000 + 300 + 10 + 6

6. Write 7,529 in expanded form.
    (A) 7,000 + 500 + 20 + 9
    (B) 7,000 + 50 + 5
    (C) 75,000 + 200 + 90
    (D) 70,000 + 5,000 + 20 + 9

7. Write 2,834 in expanded form.
    (A) 2,000 + 800 + 30 + 4
    (B) 2,000 + 80 + 8
    (C) 20,000 + 8,000 + 30 + 4
    (D) 28,000 + 300 + 40

8. Write 9,157 in expanded form.
    (A) 91,000 + 500 + 70
    (B) 90,000 + 1,000 + 50 + 7
    (C) 9,000 + 100 + 50 + 7
    (D) 9,000 + 10 + 1

9. Write 6,418 in expanded form.
    (A) 6,000 + 40 + 4
    (B) 6,000 + 400 + 10 + 8
    (C) 60,000 + 4,000 + 10 + 8
    (D) 64,000 + 100 + 80

10. Write 2,537 in expanded form.
    (A) 25,000 + 300 + 70
    (B) 2,000 + 500 + 30 + 7
    (C) 20,000 + 5,000 + 30 + 7
    (D) 2,000 + 50 + 5

Practice 13

> Numbers can also be written in expanded form using words.
> **Examples:**
> 589 is the same as 5 hundreds + 8 tens + 9 ones
> 85,901 is the same as 8 ten thousands + 5 thousands + 9 hundreds + 1 one

Write the following numbers in expanded form using words.

1. 623 _____

_____

2. 5,012 _____

_____

3. 30,968 _____

_____

4. 208 _____

_____

5. 73,997 _____

_____

6. 8,647 _____

_____

7. 356,911 _____

_____

8. 415,827 _____

_____

9. 442 _____

_____

10. 6,928 _____

_____

Write the numbers in order from least to greatest.

_____ ; _____ ; _____ ; _____ ; _____ ;

_____ ; _____ ; _____ ; _____

Practice 14 ⟳ ⟳ ⟳ ⟳ ⟳ ⟳ ⟳ ⟳ ⟳ ⟳ ⟳ ⟳ ⟳ ⟳

Read the number in written form. Then write the number in expanded form and also in standard form.

Written Form	Expanded Form	Standard Form
1. three hundred forty-two thousand, two hundred ten	300,000 + 40,000 + 2,000 + 200 + 10	342,210
2. three hundred forty-five thousand, sixteen		
3. five hundred thirty thousand, two hundred one		
4. seven hundred fifty thousand, nine hundred eleven		
5. four hundred seventy-six thousand, eight hundred twenty		
6. one hundred thousand, four hundred thirty-seven		
7. eight hundred sixty-one thousand, one hundred ninety-two		

Practice 15 ❧ ◉ ❧ ◉ ❧ ◉ ❧ ◉ ❧ ◉ ❧ ◉

1. What is the word name for 551?

   (A) five hundred fifty-one

   (B) five hundred five one

   (C) five fifty-one

   (D) five hundreds, fifty tens, and one one

2. What is the word name for 335?

   (A) three hundreds, thirty tens, and five ones

   (B) three hundred thirty-five

   (C) three thirty-five

   (D) three hundred three five

3. What is the word name for 676?

   (A) six hundred seventy-six

   (B) six hundred seven six

   (C) six seventy-six

   (D) six hundreds, seventy tens, and six ones

4. What is the word name for 717?

   (A) seven hundreds, ten tens, and seven ones

   (B) seven seventeen

   (C) seven hundred seventeen

   (D) seven hundred one seven

5. What is the word name for 168?

   (A) one sixty-eight

   (B) one hundred six eight

   (C) one hundred sixty-eight

   (D) one hundred, sixty tens, and eight ones

6. What is the word name for 993?

   (A) nine hundred nine three

   (B) nine ninety-three

   (C) nine hundred ninety-three

   (D) nine hundreds, ninety tens, and three ones

7. What is the word name for 244?

   (A) two forty-four

   (B) two hundred forty-four

   (C) two hundreds, forty tens, and four ones

   (D) two hundred four four

8. What is the word name for 829?

   (A) eight hundred two nine

   (B) eight twenty-nine

   (C) eight hundreds, twenty tens, and nine ones

   (D) eight hundred twenty-nine

9. What is the word name for 482?

   (A) four eighty-two

   (B) four hundred eighty-two

   (C) four hundred eight two

   (D) four hundreds, eighty tens, and two ones

10. What is the word name for 161?

    (A) one hundred sixty-one

    (B) one hundred six one

    (C) one hundred, sixty tens, and one one

    (D) one sixty-one

Practice 16

1. Use words to write 34,403.

   (A) thirty-four thousand, four hundred three

   (B) three hundred forty thousand, four hundred three

   (C) thirty-four, four thousand thirty

   (D) thirty-four thousand and four hundred three

2. Use words to write 29,667.

   (A) twenty-nine thousand, six hundred sixty-seven

   (B) twenty-nine thousand and six hundred sixty-seven

   (C) two hundred ninety thousand, six hundred sixty-seven

   (D) twenty-nine, six thousand six hundred seventy

3. Use words to write 65,152.

   (A) sixty-five, one thousand five hundred twenty

   (B) sixty-five thousand, one hundred fifty-two

   (C) six hundred fifty thousand, one hundred fifty-two

   (D) sixty-five thousand and one hundred fifty-two

4. Use words to write 86,192.

   (A) eighty-six, one thousand nine hundred twenty

   (B) eight hundred sixty thousand, one hundred ninety-two

   (C) eighty-six thousand, one hundred ninety-two

   (D) eighty-six thousand and one hundred ninety-two

5. Use words to write 44,163.

   (A) forty-four, one thousand six hundred thirty

   (B) forty-four thousand and one hundred sixty-three

   (C) four hundred forty thousand, one hundred sixty-three

   (D) forty-four thousand, one hundred sixty-three

6. Use words to write 24,692.

   (A) two hundred forty thousand, six hundred ninety-two

   (B) twenty-four thousand, six hundred ninety-two

   (C) twenty-four, six thousand nine hundred twenty

   (D) twenty-four thousand and six hundred ninety-two

7. Use words to write 16,407.

   (A) one hundred sixty thousand, four hundred seven

   (B) sixteen, four thousand seventy

   (C) sixteen thousand and four hundred seven

   (D) sixteen thousand, four hundred seven

8. Use words to write 46,868.

   (A) four hundred sixty thousand, eight hundred sixty-eight

   (B) forty-six thousand, eight hundred sixty-eight

   (C) forty-six, eight thousand six hundred eighty

   (D) forty-six thousand and eight hundred sixty-eight

Practice 17

1. Which group of numbers is in order from *least* to *greatest*?

(A) 102,475   186,180   277,824   413,472

(B) 186,180   277,824   413,472   102,475

(C) 413,472   277,824   186,180   102,475

(D) 277,824   413,472   102,475   186,180

2. Which group of numbers is in order from *greatest* to *least*?

(A) 347,730   471,141   139,794   195,076

(B) 195,076   347,730   471,141   139,794

(C) 139,794   195,076   347,730   471,141

(D) 471,141   347,730   195,076   139,794

3. Which group of numbers is in order from *least* to *greatest*?

(A) 136,950   237,924   305,187   470,370

(B) 470,370   305,187   237,924   136,950

(C) 237,924   305,187   470,370   136,950

(D) 305,187   470,370   136,950   237,924

4. Which group of numbers is in order from *greatest* to *least*?

(A) 348,461   416,991   127,588   165,976

(B) 416,991   348,461   165,976   127,588

(C) 127,588   165,976   348,461   416,991

(D) 165,976   348,461   416,991   127,588

5. Which group of numbers is in order from *least* to *greatest*?

(A) 169,370   279,152   434,485   106,401

(B) 279,152   434,485   106,401   169,370

(C) 434,485   279,152   169,370   106,401

(D) 106,401   169,370   279,152   434,485

6. Which group of numbers is in order from *greatest* to *least*?

(A) 112,984   189,062   338,805   410,283

(B) 338,805   410,283   112,984   189,062

(C) 410,283   338,805   189,062   112,984

(D) 189,062   338,805   410,283   112,984

7. Which group of numbers is in order from *least* to *greatest*?

(A) 181,598   262,440   488,385   123,808

(B) 123,808   181,598   262,440   488,385

(C) 262,440   488,385   123,808   181,598

(D) 488,385   262,440   181,598   123,808

8. Which group of numbers is in order from *greatest* to *least*?

(A) 132,066   237,133   350,021   387,305

(B) 237,133   350,021   387,305   132,066

(C) 350,021   387,305   132,066   237,133

(D) 387,305   350,021   237,133   132,066

9. Which group of numbers is in order from *greatest* to *least*?

(A) 248,570   274,903   443,029   116,367

(B) 116,367   248,570   274,903   443,029

(C) 274,903   443,029   116,367   248,570

(D) 443,029   274,903   248,570   116,367

10. Which group of numbers is in order from *least* to *greatest*?

(A) 139,727   225,291   330,468   455,964

(B) 225,291   330,468   455,964   139,727

(C) 330,468   455,964   139,727   225,291

(D) 455,964   330,468   225,291   139,727

Practice 18

Math has a special vocabulary that is used to describe numbers and different math processes.

When comparing 2 sets of numbers, the > (greater than) symbol or the < (less than) symbol can be used. Below are examples of how to read these math sentences.

81 > 10

81 is greater than 10.

17 < 55

17 is less than 55.

Complete each problem to show greater than or less than. (Write > or < in the spaces.)

1.	14	49	**2.**	91	47	**3.**	34	72
4.	98	39	**5.**	86	22	**6.**	57	73
7.	27	38	**8.**	48	39	**9.**	98	78
10.	57	51	**11.**	46	65	**12.**	16	69
13.	43	33	**14.**	44	87	**15.**	61	41
16.	37	49	**17.**	46	31	**18.**	95	54
19.	36	54	**20.**	32	24	**21.**	42	86
22.	24	42	**23.**	74	83	**24.**	29	76
25.	33	66	**26.**	42	67	**27.**	34	46
28.	22	52	**29.**	62	22	**30.**	89	32

Practice 19

1. Which of the following will make the statement true?

   51 > _____

   (A) 51 (B) 49

   (C) 55 (D) none of these

2. Which of the following will make the statement true?

   64 < _____

   (A) 64 (B) 67

   (C) 58 (D) none of these

3. Which of the following will make the statement true?

   54 < _____

   (A) 54 (B) 46

   (C) 56 (D) none of these

4. Which of the following will make the statement true?

   47 < _____

   (A) 47 (B) 42

   (C) 55 (D) none of these

5. Which of the following will make the statement true?

   67 > _____

   (A) 67 (B) 71

   (C) 73 (D) none of these

6. Which of the following will make the statement true?

   43 < _____

   (A) 43 (B) 48

   (C) 40 (D) none of these

7. Which of the following will make the statement true?

   56 < _____

   (A) 56 (B) 53

   (C) 58 (D) none of these

8. Which of the following will make the statement true?

   34 > _____

   (A) 34 (B) 43

   (C) 29 (D) none of these

9. Which of the following will make the statement true?

   32 < _____

   (A) 32 (B) 39

   (C) 28 (D) none of these

10. Which of the following will make the statement true?

    22 > _____

    (A) 22 (B) 28

    (C) 26 (D) none of these

Practice 20

Use the > or < symbols to compare the numbers below. Complete each sentence. The first one has already been done for you.

1. 376 (**>**) 259

_376_ is greater than _259_ .

2. 923 ( ) 675

_____ is greater than _____ .

3. 987 ( ) 255

_____ is greater than _____ .

4. 550 ( ) 777

_____ is less than _____ .

5. 800 ( ) 250

_____ is greater than _____ .

6. 205 ( ) 353

_____ is less than _____ .

7. 148 ( ) 579

_____ is less than _____ .

8. 315 ( ) 188

_____ is greater than _____ .

Ordinals are words that are used to describe location. For example: She is *fourth* in line. Fourth is the ordinal. Fourth tells where the girl is in line.

Answer the questions below.

1st   2nd   3rd   4th   5th   6th   7th   8th   9th   10th

9. The square is _____ in line.

10. The oval is _____ in line.

11. The pentagon is _____ in line.

12. The diamond is _____ in line.

13. The cube is _____ in line.

14. The star is _____ in line.

Practice 21

1. Which of the following is a true statement?

   (A) $7,259 < 5,208$

   (B) $2,515 > 5,954$

   (C) $7,277 > 3,390$

   (D) $4,526 > 8,263$

2. Which of the following is a true statement?

   (A) $2,567 > 5,037$

   (B) $2,697 < 1,830$

   (C) $4,367 < 3,628$

   (D) $9,295 > 8,610$

3. Which of the following is a true statement?

   (A) $2,181 > 9,747$

   (B) $6,371 < 4,479$

   (C) $3,817 > 5,476$

   (D) $2,400 > 1,275$

4. Which of the following is a true statement?

   (A) $5,186 > 6,071$

   (B) $7,911 > 6,368$

   (C) $8,920 < 2,640$

   (D) $6,308 < 1,468$

5. Which of the following is a true statement?

   (A) $6,515 > 8,681$

   (B) $7,852 > 2,701$

   (C) $9,210 < 4,928$

   (D) $5,451 < 1,445$

6. Which of the following is a true statement?

   (A) $5,426 < 4,105$

   (B) $4,284 < 3,310$

   (C) $7,097 > 3,450$

   (D) $6,056 < 2,474$

7. Which of the following is a true statement?

   (A) $8,999 < 8,904$

   (B) $4,187 > 7,602$

   (C) $4,459 > 8,342$

   (D) $2,737 < 9,598$

8. Which of the following is a true statement?

   (A) $6,326 < 8,095$

   (B) $5,443 < 4,309$

   (C) $1,208 > 2,866$

   (D) $1,324 > 9,235$

9. Which of the following is a true statement?

   (A) $7,020 > 8,574$

   (B) $8,210 < 1,488$

   (C) $5,994 < 9,428$

   (D) $6,193 < 1,227$

10. Which of the following is a true statement?

    (A) $5,715 < 4,983$

    (B) $1,960 > 1,889$

    (C) $1,761 > 7,867$

    (D) $4,923 > 6,343$

Practice 22

1. Which group of numbers is in the correct order from *greatest* to *least*?

    (A) 44 84 64   (B) 64 44 84

    (C) 42 49 56   (D) 56 49 42

2. Which group of numbers is in the correct order from *greatest* to *least*?

    (A) 13 23 18   (B) 18 13 23

    (C) 51 43 35   (D) 35 43 51

3. Which group of numbers is in the correct order from *greatest* to *least*?

    (A) 77 63 49   (B) 25 59 42

    (C) 42 25 59   (D) 49 63 77

4. Which group of numbers is in the correct order from *greatest* to *least*?

    (A) 294 257 220

    (B) 666 786 726

    (C) 726 666 786

    (D) 220 257 294

5. Which group of numbers is in the correct order from *greatest* to *least*?

    (A) 41 71 56   (B) 29 24 19

    (C) 19 24 29   (D) 56 41 71

6. Which group of numbers is in the correct order from *greatest* to *least*?

    (A) 38 68 53   (B) 53 38 68

    (C) 16 23 30   (D) 30 23 16

7. Which group of numbers is in the correct order from *greatest* to *least*?

    (A) 39 33 45   (B) 37 32 27

    (C) 27 32 37   (D) 33 45 39

8. Which group of numbers is in the correct order from *greatest* to *least*?

    (A) 66 57 48   (B) 48 57 66

    (C) 39 79 59   (D) 59 39 79

9. Which group of numbers is in the correct order from *greatest* to *least*?

    (A) 323 355 339

    (B) 744 758 772

    (C) 772 758 744

    (D) 339 323 355

10. Which group of numbers is in the correct order from *greatest* to *least*?

    (A) 37 49 61   (B) 49 87 68

    (C) 61 49 37   (D) 68 49 87

Practice 23 ᶚ ◖ ᶚ ᶚ ◖ ᶚ ᶚ ◖ ᶚ ◖ ᶚ ◖ ᶚ ᶚ ◖

1. What is the seventh letter in the sentence?

   "The study of sound waves is called acoustics."

   (A) y   (B) o   (C) d   (D) u

---

2. What is the fifth letter in the sentence?

   "A saline solution can be made with salt and water."

   (A) l   (B) a   (C) n   (D) i

---

3. Complete the pattern.

   _____, twenty-ninth, thirtieth, thirty-first

   (A) twenty-ninth   (B) twenty-seventh   (C) twenty-eighth   (D) thirtieth

---

4. What is the twenty-ninth letter in the sentence?

   "Chlorophyll is responsible for the green color of most plants."

   (A) e   (B) h   (C) t   (D) g

---

5. Complete the pattern.

   twenty-eighth, twenty-ninth, thirtieth, _____

   (A) thirty-first   (B) twenty-seventh   (C) twenty-ninth   (D) twenty-eighth

---

6. What is the ninth letter in the sentence?

   "The study of the motion of solid bodies in air is called aerodynamics."

   (A) f   (B) o   (C) t   (D) y

---

7. Complete the pattern.

   nineteenth, twentieth, twenty-first, _____

   (A) twentieth   (B) twenty-second   (C) nineteenth   (D) eighteenth

Practice 24

1. Ian lined up 40 dominos.

   Which domino comes 3 places **after** the tenth domino?

   _____

2. Chloe lined up 35 marbles.

   Which marble comes 7 places **before** the twenty-fourth marble?

   _____

3. Juan lined up 50 cards.

   Which card comes 6 places **after** the twenty-fifth card?

   _____

4. Megan lined up 28 markers.

   Which marker comes 8 places **before** the fifteenth card?

   _____

5. Talinda lined up 60 beads to make a necklace.

   Which number represents 2 places **before** the twenty-third bead?

   _____

6. Jonathon placed 25 toy soldiers in a row.

   Write the number that represents 7 soldiers **after** the fifth soldier in line.

   _____

Practice 25

Sometimes you will just need the general value of a number. To get it, you will round. Rounding is not the exact number, but it is close.

There are some basic rules for rounding.

> ✦ If the number is 5 or above, round up to the next tens place. For example, 26 is rounded up to 30.
>
> ✦ If the number is less than 5, round down to the last tens. For example, 13 is rounded down to 10.
>
> ✦ If the number is more than 100, round up to the nearest hundreds place for numbers bigger than 50. For example, 162 is rounded up to 200.
>
> ✦ If the number is more than 100, round down to the last hundreds place for numbers less than 50. For example, 123 is rounded down to 100.

Now it is your turn. For each number given, circle the correct rounded number.

1. 48 ➜ 40 or 50?

2. 62 ➜ 60 or 70?

3. 93 ➜ 90 or 100?

4. 15 ➜ 10 or 20?

5. 67 ➜ 60 or 70?

6. 11 ➜ 10 or 20?

7. 19 ➜ 10 or 20?

8. 408 ➜ 400 or 500?

9. 559 ➜ 500 or 600?

10. 232 ➜ 200 or 300?

11. 875 ➜ 800 or 900?

12. 845 ➜ 800 or 900?

13. 341 ➜ 300 or 400?

14. 633 ➜ 600 or 700?

15. 196 ➜ 100 or 200?

16. 255 ➜ 200 or 300?

Practice 26 ꩜ ꩜ ꩜ ꩜ ꩜ ꩜ ꩜ ꩜ ꩜ ꩜ ꩜ ꩜ ꩜

1. Round 36 to the nearest ten.
(A) 30   (B) 20   (C) 50   (D) 40

2. Round 43 to the nearest ten.
(A) 50   (B) 40   (C) 60   (D) 30

3. Round 31 to the nearest ten.
(A) 40   (B) 10   (C) 30   (D) 20

4. Round 46 to the nearest ten.
(A) 50   (B) 40   (C) 60   (D) 70

5. Round 86 to the nearest ten.
(A) 90   (B) 100   (C) 70   (D) 80

6. Round 95 to the nearest ten.
(A) 100   (B) 90   (C) 120   (D) 110

7. Round 49 to the nearest ten.
(A) 30   (B) 50   (C) 60   (D) 40

8. Round 56 to the nearest ten.
(A) 50   (B) 80   (C) 60   (D) 70

9. Round 82 to the nearest ten.
(A) 90   (B) 80   (C) 60   (D) 70

10. Round 44 to the nearest ten.
(A) 50   (B) 60   (C) 30   (D) 40

11. Round 54 to the nearest ten.
(A) 50   (B) 60   (C) 40   (D) 30

12. Round 479 to the nearest hundred.
(A) 300   (B) 500
(C) 400   (D) 480

13. Round 320 to the nearest hundred.
(A) 200   (B) 300
(C) 320   (D) 400

14. Round 183 to the nearest hundred.
(A) 180   (B) 200   (C) 100   (D) 0

15. Round 845 to the nearest hundred.
(A) 850   (B) 900
(C) 800   (D) 700

16. Round 719 to the nearest hundred.
(A) 600   (B) 720
(C) 700   (D) 800

17. Round 573 to the nearest hundred.
(A) 570   (B) 500
(C) 400   (D) 600

18. Round 232 to the nearest hundred.
(A) 230   (B) 200
(C) 300   (D) 100

19. Round 688 to the nearest hundred.
(A) 690   (B) 700
(C) 500   (D) 600

20. Round 561 to the nearest hundred.
(A) 400   (B) 500
(C) 600   (D) 560

21. Round 88 to the nearest ten.
(A) 80   (B) 100   (C) 70   (D) 90

22. Round 843 to the nearest hundred.
(A) 900   (B) 800
(C) 700   (D) 840

23. Round 49 to the nearest ten.
(A) 30   (B) 40   (C) 60   (D) 50

24. Round 55 to the nearest ten.
(A) 50   (B) 40   (C) 60   (D) 70

Practice 27 ⟲ ⟲ ⟲ ⟲ ⟲ ⟲ ⟲ ⟲ ⟲ ⟲ ⟲ ⟲ ⟲ ⟲

Solve each word problem by rounding each number to the nearest tens and then adding or subtracting. Show your work in the space provided.

1. Jason invited 39 girls and 22 boys to his party. How many children did Jason invite in all? The number 39 is rounded to 40. The number 22 is rounded to 20. (40 + 20 = 60) _60_ children in all were invited to the party.	$$\begin{array}{r} 40 \\ +\ 20 \\ \hline 60 \end{array}$$
2. Mariah bought 152 balloons, 127 party hats, and 213 candles for the party. How many party items did Mariah buy in all? Mariah bought _____ party items in all.	
3. Beau sent out 185 invitations. 87 people said "yes." The rest said "no." How many people said "no"? _____ people said "no."	
4. Lucy set out 210 green jellybeans, 315 red jellybeans, and 57 orange jellybeans. How many jellybeans did Lucy set out in all? Lucy set out _____ jellybeans in all.	
5. Sprinkles were put on 3 cupcakes. The children used 567 sprinkles in all. The first cupcake had 237 sprinkles. The second cupcake had 197. How many sprinkles did the third cupcake have? The third cupcake had _____ sprinkles.	
6. Darts were played at the party. Ben scored 222 points. Jacob scored 303 points. Elena scored 368 points. How many points were scored in all? _____ points were scored in all.	

7. Write the answers in order from least to greatest.

_____, _____, _____, _____, _____, _____,

Practice 28

Even numbers are all whole numbers that can be divided equally in half and remain whole numbers. Color the even numbers.

2	1	4	3	6	5	8	7	10	
12	9	14	11	16	13	18	15	20	
22	17	24	19	26	21	28	23	30	
32	25	34	27	36	29	38	31	40	
42	33	44	35	46	37	48	39	50	
52	41	54	43	56	45	58	47	60	
62	49	64	51	66	53	68	55	70	
72	57	74	59	76	61	78	63	80	
82	65	84	67	86	69	88	71	90	
92	73	94	75	96	77	98	79	100	

Practice 29

Odd numbers are all whole numbers that cannot be divided equally in half as whole numbers. Color the odd numbers.

1	2	3	5	4	7	9	6	11
8	13	10	12	15	14	16	17	18
19	20	21	23	22	25	27	24	29
26	31	28	30	33	32	34	35	36
37	38	39	41	40	43	45	42	47
44	49	46	48	51	50	52	53	54
55	56	57	59	58	61	63	60	65
62	67	64	66	69	68	70	71	72
73	74	75	77	76	79	81	78	83
80	85	82	84	87	86	88	89	90
91	92	93	95	94	97	99	96	100

Practice 30

1. Which is a set of odd numbers?

   (A) 8 15 16 19

   (B) 7 8 15 18

   (C) 2 9 14 17

   (D) 7 11 15 19

2. Which of the following numbers is odd?

   (A) 19   (B) 416

   (C) 142   (D) 644

3. Which of the following numbers is odd?

   (A) 302   (B) 486

   (C) 37   (D) 118

4. Which is a set of even numbers?

   (A) 2 3 14 17

   (B) 8 15 16 19

   (C) 2 12 14 20

   (D) 1 8 15 20

5. Which of the following numbers is even?

   (A) 683   (B) 311   (C) 79   (D) 50

6. Which of the following numbers is odd?

   (A) 126   (B) 240

   (C) 143   (D) 404

7. Which of the following numbers is even?

   (A) 124   (B) 995

   (C) 157   (D) 273

8. Which of the following numbers is even?

   (A) 81   (B) 915

   (C) 130   (D) 723

9. Which is a set of odd numbers?

   (A) 1 8 13 20

   (B) 2 3 12 15

   (C) 1 5 13 19

   (D) 8 13 16 19

10. Which of the following numbers is even?

    (A) 509   (B) 122

    (C) 243   (D) 151

11. Which is a set of even numbers?

    (A) 5 6 11 22

    (B) 4 7 14 13

    (C) 6 11 18 17

    (D) 4 10 14 22

12. Which of the following numbers is odd?

    (A) 642   (B) 112

    (C) 113   (D) 878

13. Which is a set of odd numbers?

    (A) 4 3 18 9   (B) 6 7 20 13

    (C) 1 6 7 22   (D) 1 5 7 13

14. Which of the following numbers is even?

    (A) 937   (B) 38   (C) 319   (D) 55

Practice 31

---

1. Write the missing numbers.

5,491; _____ ; 5,493

8,190; _____ ; 8,192

2. Write the missing numbers.

_____ ; 9,287; 9,290

_____ ; 9,430; 9,440

3. Write the missing numbers.

4,672; _____ ; 4,676

6,565; _____ ; 6,575

---

4. Complete the pattern.

7,623; 7,723; 7,823; _____ ; _____ ;

_____ ; _____ ; _____ ; _____ ;

_____

5. Complete the pattern.

4,183; 4,193; 4,203; _____ ; _____ ;

_____ ; _____ ; _____ ; _____ ;

_____

---

6. In which place is the 8?

836,914

_____

7. In which place is the 2?

602,880

_____

8. In which place is the 0?

980,733

_____

---

9. Write the number in standard form.

One hundred ninety-two thousand, three hundred forty-six

_____

10. Write the number in standard form.

Eight hundred thousand, six hundred one

_____

Practice 32

Label four cups as shown. Place a six-sided or nine-sided die in each cup.

Shake the cups. Record the numbers shown on the die in each cup on the recording sheet below. In the last column, write the place value of the number marked with a ★.

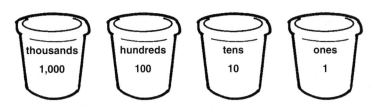

	thousands	hundreds	tens	ones	★ place of selected number
1.	3 ,	8 ★	7	1	hundreds
2.	★ ,				
3.	,			★	
4.	,		★		
5.	,		★		
6.	,	★			
7.	★ ,				
8.	,			★	
9.	★ ,				
10.	★ ,				

11. Write the starred numbers in order from smallest to largest.

_____, _____, _____, _____, _____, _____, _____, _____, _____, _____

12. What was the largest number made? _____

13. What was the smallest number made? _____

14. Write the odd numbers that were made.

_____

15. Write the even numbers that were made.

_____

Practice 33

Number 50 index cards from 0–9. Shuffle the number cards and place them in a stack facedown. Turn over the top five cards and lay them out in the order they were turned over. Record the numbers. Write whether the number made is odd or even. (Remember, odd numbers end in 1, 3, 5, 7, or 9 and even numbers end in 0, 2, 4, 6, or 8.) Write the numbers that come before and after the number made. The first one has been done for you.

	number made with the cards	odd or even	number that comes before	number that comes after
1.	3 6 , 9 0 8	even	36,907	36,909
2.				
3.				
4.				
5.				
6.				
7.				
8.				
9.				
10.				

Practice 34

The data in the box below is taken from dietary sheets provided by McDonald's restaurants. Read through the Data box and use the information provided to figure out which side of each inequality has the greater number of calories. Place a < or > sign in the space provided to complete each problem.

Data

These figures reflect the number of calories in each item.

 hamburger—270

 cheeseburger—320

 fish sandwich—360

 small French fries—210

garden salad—80

 hot fudge sundae—290

 apple pie—260

 1% milk—100

 small cola—150

 chocolate shake—340

1. 2 hamburgers _____ 2 hot fudge sundaes

2. 1 fish sandwich _____ 4 garden salads

3. 5 small colas _____ 3 fish sandwiches

4. 3 chocolate shakes _____ 12 1% milks

5. 2 apple pies _____ 7 garden salads

6. 3 cheeseburgers _____ 5 small French fries

7. 2 garden salads + 3 cheeseburgers _____ 4 hamburgers

8. 4 fish sandwiches _____ 6 small French fries + 1 garden salad

9. 2 small colas + 1 chocolate shake _____ 2 apple pies + 3 1% milks

10. 2 hot fudge sundaes _____ 2 small French fries + 3 garden salads

11. 6 1% milks + 2 cheeseburgers _____ 4 small French fries + 1 shake

12. 2 apple pies + 2 fish sandwiches _____ 3 cheeseburgers + 3 small French fries

In the space below write two more inequalities using the data from the box above.

1. _____

2. _____

Practice 35 ᕽ ᕽ ᕽ ᕽ ᕽ ᕽ ᕽ ᕽ ᕽ ᕽ ᕽ ᕽ ᕽ ᕽ ᕽ ᕽ ᕽ

Read each clue. Put an "X" on the number(s) that do not fit each clue. After answering all of the clues, there will be one number left.

805,457	**879**	**80,121**	**579**
2,157	**39,643**	**29,253**	**144,384**
66,175	**9,780**	**7,418**	**102**

Clues

1. When my digits are added together, the total is a number between 20 through 30.

2. There is one 7 in my number.

3. There are more than 3 digits in my number.

4. If you add and subtract each number in order, the answer is less than 10.
   (**Example:** 579, 5 + 7 − 9 = 3)

5. I have more odd digits than even digits.

6. Which number am I? _____

7. Write a clue that would fit the mystery number. _____

_____

_____

_____

Practice 36

Arabic and Roman numerals are ways of writing numbers. Arabic numerals are used throughout the world and look like this: 1, 2, 3, 60, 71, etc. Roman numerals are also used throughout the world and are often used to show the year that a movie was made or a book was published. Roman numerals look like this: I, V, X, L, C, etc.

Arabic	1	2	3	4	5	6	7	8	9
Roman	I	II	III	IV	V	VI	VII	VIII	IX

Arabic	10	11	12	13	14	15	16	17	18	19
Roman	X	XI	XII	XIII	XIV	XV	XVI	XVII	XVIII	XIX

Arabic	20	30	40	50	60	70	80	90	100
Roman	XX	XXX	XL	L	LX	LXX	LXXX	XC	C

Arabic	150	200	300	400	500	600	700	800	900	1000
Roman	CL	CC	CCC	CD	D	DC	DCC	DCCC	CM	M

Directions: Write the following numbers using Roman numerals. Use the chart above to help you.

1. 27 _____

2. 75 _____

3. 890 _____

4. 950 _____

5. 2000 _____

6. 650 _____

7. 62 _____

8. 56 _____

9. 110 _____

10. 370 _____

11. 98 _____

12. 240 _____

Challenge: Write the year you were born in Arabic numerals and then in Roman numerals.

Arabic _____   Roman _____

Test Practice 1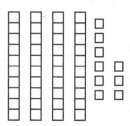

1. Which number matches the blocks below?

(A) 71   **(B)** 26   **(C)** 72   **(D)** 27

2. Which number matches the blocks below?

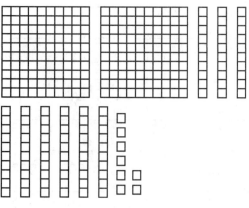

(A) 299   **(B)** 298

(C) 290   **(D)** 289

3. What place value does the digit 8 have in 2,853?

(A) tens   **(B)** hundreds

(C) ones   **(D)** sixties

4. What is the value of the digit 4 in the number 6,784?

(A) 4   **(B)** 400   **(C)** 40   **(D)** 1

5. Write $600,000 + 10,000 + 2,000 + 90 + 8$ in standard form.

(A) 612,089   **(B)** 6,120,098

(C) 61,298   **(D)** 612,098

6. Which number matches the blocks below?

(A) 94   **(B)** 48   **(C)** 49   **(D)** 95

7. What place value does the digit 5 have in 5,368?

(A) tens   **(B)** five hundreds

(C) ones   **(D)** thousands

8. Write $900 + 20 + 3$ in standard form.

(A) 329   **(B)** 950

(C) 923   **(D)** 932

9. Write $400,000 + 50,000 + 5,000 + 700 + 40 + 1$ in standard form.

(A) 455,741   **(B)** 4,557,041

(C) 4,055,741   **(D)** 455,714

10. Write $100,000 + 60,000 + 7,000 + 900 + 30 + 6$ in standard form.

(A) 1,679,036   **(B)** 167,963

(C) 1,067,936   **(D)** 167,936

11. Write $600 + 90 + 5$ in standard form.

(A) 695   **(B)** 659

(C) 596   **(D)** 740

Test Practice 2

1. What is the word name for 781?

   (A) seven hundreds, eighty tens, and one one

   (B) seven hundred eight one

   (C) seven hundred eighty-one

   (D) seven eighty-one

2. What is the word name for 859?

   (A) eight hundred fifty-nine

   (B) eight hundreds, fifty tens, and nine ones

   (C) eight fifty-nine

   (D) eight hundred five nine

3. Which of the following will make the statement true?

   42 < _____

   (A) 45　　　　　(B) 42

   (C) 38　　　　　(D) none of these

4. Which of the following is a true statement?

   (A) 6,007 < 1,842

   (B) 1,723 > 3,263

   (C) 2,513 > 1,239

   (D) 5,661 < 4,653

5. Which group of numbers is in the correct order from *greatest* to *least*?

   (A) 67　50　84　　(B) 34　43　52

   (C) 50　84　67　　(D) 52　43　34

6. Which of the following numbers is odd?

   (A) 57　　　　　(B) 930

   (C) 312　　　　(D) 200

7. Which of the following numbers is even?

   (A) 181　　　　(B) 363

   (C) 917　　　　(D) 42

8. Which of the following will make the statement true?

   74 > _____

   (A) 74　　　　　(B) 78

   (C) 69　　　　　(D) none of these

9. Which of the following will make the statement true?

   62 > _____

   (A) 68　　　　　(B) 53

   (C) 62　　　　　(D) none of these

10. Which of the following is a true statement?

    (A) 3,776 > 5,623

    (B) 2,393 < 1,128

    (C) 3,246 > 8,932

    (D) 1,739 < 3,482

11. Which group of numbers is in the correct order from *greatest* to *least*?

    (A) 27　59　43　　(B) 58　47　36

    (C) 43　27　59　　(D) 36　47　58

12. Which is a set of odd numbers?

    (A) 4　15　12　19

    (B) 5　13　15　19

    (C) 5　4　15　18

    (D) 2　7　8　17

Test Practice 3 ⟳ ⟳ ⟳ ⟳ ⟳ ⟳ ⟳ ⟳ ⟳ ⟳ ⟳ ⟳

1. What is another way to write 3 thousands 9 tens 4 ones?

(A) 394

(B) 3,094

(C) 3,904

(D) 3,940

2. In which number does the 8 stand for 8 hundreds?

(A) 1,584

(B) 4,518

(C) 5,814

(D) 8,541

3. Which number is greater than 6,979?

(A) 6,798

(B) 6,978

(C) 6,879

(D) 6,987

4. 984 rounded to the nearest ten is . . .

(A) 900

(B) 980

(C) 990

(D) 1,000

5. Which is the expanded form of 7,230?

(A) 700 + 20 + 3

(B) 700 + 200 + 30

(C) 7,000 + 20 + 3

(D) 7,000 + 200 + 30

6. To estimate the sum of 8,372 and 7,931 to the nearest thousand, you should add . . .

(A) 7,000 and 7,000

(B) 8,000 and 7,000

(C) 8,000 and 8,000

(D) 8,000 and 9,000

7. Which is the numeral for six thousand eighty-seven?

(A) 687

(B) 6,087

(C) 60,087

(D) 687,000

8. What is the value of the 5 in 654,732?

(A) 500

(B) 5,000

(C) 50,000

(D) 500,000

9. 568,291 rounded to the nearest thousand is?

(A) 560,000

(B) 568,200

(C) 568,000

(D) 570,000

10. Which is the standard form for 6 hundreds 7 ones?

(A) 67

(B) 607

(C) 670

(D) 6,007

Test Practice 4

1. What is the twelfth letter of the alphabet?

(A) F

(B) L

(C) G

(D) N

2. Which number would be thirty if rounded to the nearest 10?

(A) 22

(B) 24

(C) 26

(D) 39

3. What number is missing from this number pattern?

61, 57, 53, _____ , 45, 41

(A) 51

(B) 52

(C) 47

(D) 49

4. Which answer shows counting by fives?

(A) 5, 9, 13, 17

(B) 20, 25, 30, 35

(C) 6, 12, 18, 24

(D) 1, 3, 5, 7

5. What is the Roman numeral for 19?

(A) XIX

(B) XXI

(C) XVIIII

(D) VVVIIII

6. This function table shows input numbers and output numbers. The rule used to change the numbers from input to output is shown above the table. Which number is missing from the table?

Rule: Add 3 and then multiply by 2.

Input	Output
2	10
6	?
10	26

(A) 12

(B) 18

(C) 16

(D) 20

7. To what number is the arrow pointing?

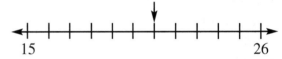

(A) 17

(B) 19

(C) 21

(D) 25

8. Find the number that is missing from this number pattern.

425, 420, 415, _____, 405

(A) 400

(B) 395

(C) 305

(D) 410

Test Practice 5

1. What is another way to write a number which is 4 thousands, 8 tens, and 2 ones?

   (A) 482
   (C) 40,082
   (B) 4,082
   (D) 4,182

2. To estimate the sum of 4,215 and 6,957 to the nearest thousand, you should add

   (A) 5,000 and 7,000
   (B) 4,000 and 7,000
   (C) 4,000 and 6,000
   (D) 5,000 and 5,000

3. In which number does the 7 stand for hundreds?

   (A) 7,512
   (C) 3,741
   (B) 5,173
   (D) 6,337

4. Which number is > 5,836?

   (A) 5,880
   (C) 5,835
   (B) 5,386
   (D) 5,737

5. The newspaper said about 495 people attended a horse show. If the newspaper were rounding to the nearest hundred, about how many people attended the horse show?

   (A) 550
   (B) 500
   (C) 400
   (D) 450

6. Round 21 to the nearest ten. Round 37 to the nearest ten. Multiply these two rounded numbers. The answer is

   (A) 90
   (C) 1,000
   (B) 800
   (D) 600

7. Round the numbers in the problem to the nearest ten to estimate the answer.

   $$22 + 18 =$$

   (A) 20
   (C) 60
   (B) 40
   (D) 50

8. What is the value of 4 in 348,371?

   (A) 400
   (B) 4,000
   (C) 40,000
   (D) 400,000

9. Which is the largest?

   (A) 4.91
   (C) 4.910
   (B) 49.1
   (D) 4,910

10. What is the next number in this series: 30, 300, 3000, _____.

    (A) 3,003
    (C) 30,000
    (B) 900
    (D) 300,000

11. If you add a zero after the 2 in the number 392, the new number is

    (A) three thousand one hundred and ninety-two.
    (B) three thousand nine hundred two.
    (C) three thousand ninety-two.
    (D) three thousand nine hundred twenty.

12. What is this number rounded to the nearest ten: eight hundred eighty-nine.

    (A) 889
    (C) 899
    (B) 890
    (D) 900

13. Which is the numeral for four thousand seventy-three?

    (A) 4,173
    (C) 40,073
    (B) 4,073
    (D) 4,730

14. Round the numbers in the problem to the nearest hundred to estimate the answer.

    $$\begin{array}{r} 222 \\ + 888 \\ \hline \end{array}$$

    (A) 1,000
    (B) 1,100
    (C) 1,010
    (D) 1,110

Test Practice 6

1. What number is needed to make this number sentence true?

$55 - \boxed{} = 19$

(A) 30

(B) 34

(C) 36

(D) 74

2. Which sign will correctly complete this number sentence?

$9 \boxed{} 7 = 16$

(A) +

(B) –

(C) x

(D) ÷

3. What number is missing from this number sentence?

$\boxed{} \times 8 = 48$

(A) 5

(B) 6

(C) 7

(D) 56

4. Which sign will make this number sentence true?

$9 \boxed{} 4 = 2 + 3$

(A) +

(B) –

(C) x

(D) ÷

5. Which sign will make this number sentence true?

$24 \boxed{} 6 = 2 \times 2$

(A) +

(B) –

(C) x

(D) ÷

6. Which sign will make this number sentence true?

$30 \boxed{} 3 = 90$

(A) +

(B) –

(C) x

(D) ÷

7. What number goes in the box to make this sentence true?

$\boxed{} \div 8 = 7$

(A) 49

(B) 56

(C) 63

(D) 64

8. What number will make this number sentence true?

$6 + 24 + \boxed{} = 45$

(A) 5

(B) 10

(C) 15

(D) 20

Answer Sheet

Test Practice 1

1. Ⓐ Ⓑ Ⓒ Ⓓ
2. Ⓐ Ⓑ Ⓒ Ⓓ
3. Ⓐ Ⓑ Ⓒ Ⓓ
4. Ⓐ Ⓑ Ⓒ Ⓓ
5. Ⓐ Ⓑ Ⓒ Ⓓ
6. Ⓐ Ⓑ Ⓒ Ⓓ
7. Ⓐ Ⓑ Ⓒ Ⓓ
8. Ⓐ Ⓑ Ⓒ Ⓓ
9. Ⓐ Ⓑ Ⓒ Ⓓ
10. Ⓐ Ⓑ Ⓒ Ⓓ
11. Ⓐ Ⓑ Ⓒ Ⓓ

Test Practice 2

1. Ⓐ Ⓑ Ⓒ Ⓓ
2. Ⓐ Ⓑ Ⓒ Ⓓ
3. Ⓐ Ⓑ Ⓒ Ⓓ
4. Ⓐ Ⓑ Ⓒ Ⓓ
5. Ⓐ Ⓑ Ⓒ Ⓓ
6. Ⓐ Ⓑ Ⓒ Ⓓ
7. Ⓐ Ⓑ Ⓒ Ⓓ
8. Ⓐ Ⓑ Ⓒ Ⓓ
9. Ⓐ Ⓑ Ⓒ Ⓓ
10. Ⓐ Ⓑ Ⓒ Ⓓ
11. Ⓐ Ⓑ Ⓒ Ⓓ
12. Ⓐ Ⓑ Ⓒ Ⓓ

Test Practice 3

1. Ⓐ Ⓑ Ⓒ Ⓓ
2. Ⓐ Ⓑ Ⓒ Ⓓ
3. Ⓐ Ⓑ Ⓒ Ⓓ
4. Ⓐ Ⓑ Ⓒ Ⓓ
5. Ⓐ Ⓑ Ⓒ Ⓓ
6. Ⓐ Ⓑ Ⓒ Ⓓ
7. Ⓐ Ⓑ Ⓒ Ⓓ
8. Ⓐ Ⓑ Ⓒ Ⓓ
9. Ⓐ Ⓑ Ⓒ Ⓓ
10. Ⓐ Ⓑ Ⓒ Ⓓ

Test Practice 4

1. Ⓐ Ⓑ Ⓒ Ⓓ
2. Ⓐ Ⓑ Ⓒ Ⓓ
3. Ⓐ Ⓑ Ⓒ Ⓓ
4. Ⓐ Ⓑ Ⓒ Ⓓ
5. Ⓐ Ⓑ Ⓒ Ⓓ
6. Ⓐ Ⓑ Ⓒ Ⓓ
7. Ⓐ Ⓑ Ⓒ Ⓓ
8. Ⓐ Ⓑ Ⓒ Ⓓ

Test Practice 5

1. Ⓐ Ⓑ Ⓒ Ⓓ
2. Ⓐ Ⓑ Ⓒ Ⓓ
3. Ⓐ Ⓑ Ⓒ Ⓓ
4. Ⓐ Ⓑ Ⓒ Ⓓ
5. Ⓐ Ⓑ Ⓒ Ⓓ
6. Ⓐ Ⓑ Ⓒ Ⓓ
7. Ⓐ Ⓑ Ⓒ Ⓓ
8. Ⓐ Ⓑ Ⓒ Ⓓ
9. Ⓐ Ⓑ Ⓒ Ⓓ
10. Ⓐ Ⓑ Ⓒ Ⓓ
11. Ⓐ Ⓑ Ⓒ Ⓓ
12. Ⓐ Ⓑ Ⓒ Ⓓ
13. Ⓐ Ⓑ Ⓒ Ⓓ
14. Ⓐ Ⓑ Ⓒ Ⓓ

Test Practice 6

1. Ⓐ Ⓑ Ⓒ Ⓓ
2. Ⓐ Ⓑ Ⓒ Ⓓ
3. Ⓐ Ⓑ Ⓒ Ⓓ
4. Ⓐ Ⓑ Ⓒ Ⓓ
5. Ⓐ Ⓑ Ⓒ Ⓓ
6. Ⓐ Ⓑ Ⓒ Ⓓ
7. Ⓐ Ⓑ Ⓒ Ⓓ
8. Ⓐ Ⓑ Ⓒ Ⓓ

Answer Key

Page 4
1. A
2. A
3. C
4. A
5. C
6. B

Page 5
1. A
2. B
3. D
4. B
5. D
6. C

Page 6
1. 194
2. 362
3. 98
4. 422
5. 503
6. 501
7. 272
8. 486

Page 7
1. 263
2. 526
3. 340
4. 458
5. 601

Page 8
1. B
2. A
3. D
4. C
5. D
6. B
7. C
8. A
9. B
10. A

Page 9
1. A
2. A
3. B
4. C
5. D
6. C
7. D
8. B
9. B
10. D

Page 10
1. 6
2. 6
3. 7
4. 4
5. 2
6. 5
7. 4
8. 5
9. 4
10. 6
11. hundreds
12. ones
13. tens
14. ten thousands
15. thousands
16. hundred thousands
17. ten thousands
18. ones
19. tens
20. hundred-thousands

Page 11
1. C
2. D
3. B
4. A
5. B
6. C
7. D
8. C
9. C
10. A
11. C
12. D
13. C
14. D
15. B
16. A
17. B
18. C

Page 12
1. C
2. D
3. D
4. A
5. C
6. B
7. B
8. B
9. A
10. C

Page 13
1. 45,358
2. 28,965
3. 64,747
4. 96,576
5. 78,399
6. 59,232
7. 24,623
8. 73,884
9. 62,973
10. 57,396

Page 14
1. B
2. B
3. D
4. D
5. C
6. C
7. B
8. B
9. D
10. D

Page 15
1. D
2. B
3. D
4. D
5. D
6. A
7. A
8. C
9. B
10. B

Page 16
1. 6 hundreds + 2 tens + 3 ones
2. 5 thousands + 1 ten + 2 ones
3. 3 ten thousands + 9 hundreds + 6 tens + 8 ones
4. 2 hundreds + 8 ones
5. 7 ten thousands + 3 thousands + 9 hundreds + 9 tens + 7 ones
6. 8 thousands + 6 hundreds + 4 tens + 7 ones
7. 3 hundred thousands + 5 ten thousands + 6 thousands + 9 hundreds + 1 ten + 1 one
8. 4 hundred thousands + 1 ten thousand + 5 thousands + 8 hundreds + 2 tens + 7 ones
9. 4 hundreds + 4 tens + 2 ones
10. 6 thousands + 9 hundreds + 2 tens + 8 ones

Number order:
208; 442; 623; 5,012; 6,928; 8,647; 30,968; 73,997; 356,911; 415,827

Page 17
1. 300,000 + 40,000 + 2,000 + 200 + 10; 342,210
2. 300,000 + 40,000 + 5,000 + 10 + 6; 345,016
3. 500,000 + 30,000 + 200 + 1; 530,201
4. 700,000 + 50,000 + 900 + 10 + 1; 750,911
5. 400,000 + 70,000 + 6,000 + 800 + 20; 476,820
6. 100,000 + 400 + 30 + 7; 100,437
7. 800,000 + 60,000 + 1,000 + 100 + 90 + 2; 861,192

Page 18
1. A
2. B
3. A
4. C
5. C
6. C
7. B
8. D
9. B
10. A

Page 19
1. A
2. A
3. B
4. C
5. D
6. B
7. D
8. B

Page 20
1. A
2. D
3. A
4. B
5. D
6. C
7. B
8. D
9. D
10. A

Page 21
1. <
2. >
3. <
4. >
5. >
6. <
7. <
8. >
9. >
10. >
11. <
12. <
13. >
14. <
15. >
16. <
17. >
18. >
19. <
20. >
21. <
22. <
23. <
24. <
25. <
26. <
27. <
28. <
29. >
30. >

Page 22
1. B
2. B
3. C
4. C
5. D
6. B
7. C
8. C
9. B
10. D

Page 23
1. 376 > 259; 376 is greater than 259.
2. 923 > 675; 923 is greater than 675.
3. 987 > 255; 987 is greater than 255.
4. 550 < 777; 550 is less than 777.
5. 800 > 250; 800 is greater than 250.
6. 205 < 353; 205 is less than 353.
7. 148 < 579; 148 is less than 579.
8. 315 > 188; 315 is greater than 188.
9. 1st
10. 5th
11. 10th
12. 6th
13. 9th
14. 3rd

Answer Key

Page 24
1. C
2. D
3. D
4. B
5. B
6. C
7. D
8. A
9. C
10. B

Page 25
1. D
2. C
3. A
4. A
5. B
6. D
7. B
8. A
9. C
10. C

Page 26
1. C
2. D
3 C
4. B
5. A
6. B
7. B

Page 27
1. thirteenth
2. seventeenth
3. thirty-first
4. seventh
5. twenty-first
6. twelve

Page 28
1. 50
2. 60
3. 90
4. 20
5. 70
6. 10
7. 20
8. 400
9. 600
10. 200
11. 900
12. 800
13. 300
14. 600
15. 200
16. 300

Page 29
1. D
2. B
3. C
4. A
5. A
6. A
7. B
8. C
9. B
10. D
11. A
12. B
13. B
14. B
15. C
16. C
17. D
18. B
19. B
20. C
21. D
22. B
23. D
24. C

Page 30
1. 40 + 20 = 60; 60 children were invited to the party.
2. 150 + 130 + 210 = 490; Mariah bought 490 items in all.
3. 190 – 90 = 100; 100 people said "no."
4. 210 + 320 + 60 = 590; Lucy set out 590 jellybeans.
5. 570 – 240 = 330; - 200 = 130; The third cupcake had 130 sprinkles.
6. 220 + 300 + 370 = 890; 890 points were scored in all.

Page 31
2, 4, 6, 8, 10, 12, 14, 16, 18, 20, 22, 24, 26, 28, 30, 32, 34, 36, 38, 40, 42, 44, 46, 48, 50, 52, 54, 56, 58, 60 62, 64, 66, 68, 70, 72, 74, 76. 78. 80, 82, 84, 86, 88, 90, 92, 94, 96, 98, 100

Page 32
1. 1, 3, 5, 7, 9, 11, 13, 15, 17, 19, 21, 23, 25, 27, 29, 31, 33, 35, 37, 39, 41, 43, 45, 47, 49, 51, 53, 55, 57, 59, 61, 53, 65, 67, 69, 71, 73, 75, 77, 79, 81, 83, 85, 87, 89, 91, 93, 95, 97, 99

Page 33
1. D
2. A
3. C
4. C
5. D
6. C
7. A
8. C
9. C
10. B
11. D
12. C
13. D
14. B

Page 34
1. 5,492
8,191
2. 9,284
9,420
3. 4,674
6,570
4. 7,923; 8,023; 8,123; 8,223; 8,323; 8,423; 8,523
5. 4,213; 4,223; 4,233; 4,243; 4,253; 4,263; 4,273
6. hundred thousands
7. thousands
8. thousands
9. 192,346
10. 800,601

Page 35 and 36
1. Answers will vary.

Page 37
1. <
2. >
3. <
4. <
5. <
6. <
7. >
8. >
9. <
10. <
11. >
12. <

Page 38
1. cross off 2,157; 80,121; 7,418; 102
2. cross off 39,643; 29,253; 144,384
3. cross off 879; 579
4. cross off 66,175
5. cross off 9,780
6. 805,457
7. Answers will vary.

Page 39
1. XXVII
2. LXXV
3. DCCCXC
4. CML
5. MM
6. DCL
7. LXII
8. LVI
9. CX
10. CCCLXX
11. XCVIII
12. CCXL

Page 40
1. D
2. B
3. B
4. A
5. D
6. C
7. D
8. C
9. A
10. D
11. A

Page 41
1. C
2. A
3. A
4. C
5. D
6. A
7. D
8. C
9. B
10. D
11. B
12. B

Page 42
1. B
2. C
3. D
4. B
5. D
6. C
7. B
8. C
9. C
10. B

Page 43
1. B
2. C
3. D
4. B
5. A
6. B
7. C
8. D

Page 44
1. B
2. B
3. C
4. A
5. B
6. B
7. B
8. C
9. D
10. C
11. D
12. B
13. B
14. B

Page 45
1. C
2. A
3. B
4. B
5. D
6. C
7. B
8. C